SWIM

ELLEN VAN NEERVEN

CURRENCY PRESS
The performing arts publisher

**GRIFFIN
THEATRE
COMPANY**

CURRENT THEATRE SERIES

First published in 2024
by Currency Press Pty Ltd,
Gadigal Land, Suite 310, 46–56 Kippax Street, Surry Hills, NSW 2010, Australia
enquiries@currency.com.au
www.currency.com.au

in association with Griffin Theatre Company

Copyright: *swim* © Ellen van Neerven, 2024.

COPYING FOR EDUCATIONAL PURPOSES

The Australian *Copyright Act 1968* [Act] allows a maximum of one chapter or 10% of this book, whichever is the greater, to be copied by any educational institution for its educational purposes provided that that educational institution [or the body that administers it] has given a remuneration notice to Copyright Agency [CA] under the Act.

For details of the CA licence for educational institutions contact CA,

12 / 66 Goulburn Street, Sydney, NSW, 2000; tel: within Australia 1800 066 844 toll free; outside Australia 61 2 9394 7600; fax: 61 2 9394 7601; email: memberservices@copyright.com.au

COPYING FOR OTHER PURPOSES

Except as permitted under the Act, for example a fair dealing for the purposes of study, research, criticism or review, no part of this book may be reproduced, stored in a retrieval system, or transmitted in any form or by any means without prior written permission. All enquiries should be made to the publisher at the address above.

Any performance or public reading of *swim* is forbidden unless a licence has been received from the author or the author's agent. The purchase of this book in no way gives the purchaser the right to perform the play in public, whether by means of a staged production or a reading. All applications for public performance should be addressed to the author c /—Currency Press at the address above.

Typeset by Brighton Gray for Currency Press.
Cover image shows Dani Sib; photo by Daniel Grant; cover design by Susu Studio.

Currency Press acknowledges the Traditional Owners of the Country on which we live and work. We pay our respects to all Aboriginal and Torres Strait Islander Elders, past and present.

A catalogue record for this book is available from the National Library of Australia

Contents

SWIM

    Part One: Changing Room   3

    Part Two: Pool   13

    Part Three: Transformation Room   53

Theatre Program at the end of the playtext

swim was first produced by Griffin Theatre Company at Carriageworks, Gadigal Country, Sydney, on 10 July 2024, with the following cast:

E	Dani Sib
SAMENA, AUNTY	Sandy Greenwood

Director, Andrea James
Movement Director, Kirk Page
Designer, Romanie Harper
Lighting Designer, Karen Norris
Composer & Sound Designer, Brendon Boney
Video Designer, Samuel James
Cultural Consultant, Aunty Jenny Fraser
Cultural Consultant, Lann Levinge
Cultural Consultant, Aunty Maria van Neerven
Gender & Inclusivity Consultant, Bayley Turner
Stage Manager, Isabella Kerdijk
Production Manager, Damion Holling
Senior Producer, Elinor King
Associate Producer, Cassie Hamilton
Associate Producer, Paris Mordecai
Workshop Dramaturg, Bryan Andy
Workshop Choreographer, Yolande Brown
Workshop Performer, Hannah Donnelly

CHARACTERS

E, (they/them), a Murri gender-non-conforming/genderfluid person in their twenties.

SAMENA, (she/her), a Blak woman in her twenties. She works at the pool and is also DJing the play.

AUNTY, (she/her), a 50-something maternal figure who knows rivers like blood.

NOTE ON CASTING

One person plays E while a supporting role plays SAMENA/AUNTY and other roles.

PLACE/TIME

Present day. A local swimming pool.

This play text went to press before the end of rehearsals and may differ from the play as performed.

PROLOGUE

Faint singing and tap sticks.
E *sits in a gundal (dugout canoe) on dry land.*

Do you have a memory for water?
The kind that sits on your tongue
The kind that slides down your throat
The kind that gasps in your stomach

Dry mouth.
Thirst.
Cracking.
Croaking.
Especially at night.

Water marks on trees
A memory of water
that was too much and too fast
and ultimately not enough
the taste of salt.

Water
used to feel like rainbows

Water
used to flow like love

I hear an old song
On the river
In front of the mountain

Calling me closer
Closer to home
Closer to bone
Closer to the answer

Closer to the ancestors
Closer to the sound

I want this gundal
To follow the old song
flow forest to sea
But it won't move

After rain, tea tree flowers bloom.
There are some parts of Country that are never dry

Why did I stop swimming?
How can I get flowing again?

PART ONE: CHANGING ROOM

SCENE 1: ENTER

E *stands, swimming bag on their arm.*
towel around their shoulders, thongs on.

Aunty drops me off
I fish out a card
from the guts
of my swimming bag
all torn up
in pieces
try to put it back together
I hand it to the girl
at the counter
Samena, on her name tag
she says 'I haven't seen one of these for a long time
we don't have those anymore
it's all digital now. A tap key.
Just tap here,
you haven't been here for a while
have you?'
she knows
I seem out of place which is so funny
cos this used to be my place!
I scraggle around in my pockets
For loose change
Can't find any
and I look down
to her sneaks
she is wearing
socks with pink sharks on them
'don't worry about it.

your first swim's on us'
Samena is smiling and handing me a new card
a key to a locker
and I want to ask
where she got the socks
with pink sharks on them
they are cute
she flicks her big bouncy hair off her neck
and points out the doors to
two change rooms
one on the left, and one on the right
I want to say something
but my voice is numb
and I just shuffle quickly away
I move right and
the gate clicks behind me
clips me on the way
I walk a few hurried steps
to this door
to this Lady.

> *Printed on the door of the change room is a big intruding woman sign.*

What's a nice girl like you
doing in a place like this?

> E *moves around the door*
>
> *checking themself*
>
> *looking at their body*
>
> E *takes a few steps back.*
> *They look behind them.*
> *And then at the sign again.*
> *They touch the sign.*
> *Ocean. Gull calls. Wind. Waves.*
> *The door fills with water.*
> E *jumps in.*

SCENE 2: CHECK

E *finds themselves in a change room with a sea of women in it.*

I don't remember the change room being this full on
It's like the boxing day sales in here.
White women, seriously!

They do that check
when I'm coming in
and they're coming out
The check, you know what I'm talking about.
Eyes look at me: up, down, sideways
Check
then up to the sign of the door.
Check
Yes. Definitely the *Women's* change room
They didn't make a mistake.
Do they think I belong here?
They check me again. Slowly.
Check.
Their eyes narrow in on me.
and their mouths open so wide
you can fit a family of flies in there and then they say.

  E *talks in the voices of the women.*

WOMAN 1: 'Isn't that a bloke?'
WOMAN 2: 'Are you in the wrong place?'
YOUNGER WOMAN: 'Mum … stop staring.'
OLDER WOMAN: 'I'm just wondering if that's a boy or a girl that's all.'
YOUNGER WOMAN: 'Shhh. They can hear you.'

They get all quiet when I walk closer.
They bring their purse to the *other* side. Seriously?

  E *talks in the women's voices again*

WOMAN 1: 'Hey. That's *my* locker, actually.'

WOMAN 2: 'I'm holding this space for a friend.'
WOMAN 3: 'My towel is over the bench so it can dry.'
WOMAN 4: 'I'm resting my leg on the seat.'

Fine!
So I take a step back at every comment I hear or don't hear
(Bloke! Dyke! Darkie! Freak!)
And I weave and dance
between a sea of women coming and going
dodging the pointed looks
ducking under the unkind words
shrinking myself until it hurts too much
And I have to push, push, push myself
To move forward!
Find my space!

sorry I
didn't mean to
get in your way
just tryna find a dry spot
to put my shit down
in this sea of towels, legs, butts, and bras
maybe there

this used to be my special place
five a.m. five p.m. every day.
now it just sounds like sorry

tryna find my space
maybe by that wall
tryna find my space
maybe there
tryna find our space
on stolen land

    E *finds a space on a bench and guards it with their life.*

You white women, seriously! So free with your bodies
treating this room like your bedroom

prancing around in your underwear
Zips unzipping everywhere
Deodorant flying in my face
Wet togs dropping at my feet
this old girl she's letting it all hang out in my face.
Like right here.

Please. I'm not perving.
Swear to god.
I'm just trying to know where to rest my eyes
With all this action
Trying to find my bit of privacy
Coz you're definitely not getting a show back
help a Murri out wouldya
just don't look
when I take it all off

SCENE 3: MIRROR

E *sits fully clothed on a bench with their towel over their head enclosed by mirrors.*

E *removes the towel.*

Finally I'm alone.
This smells like it hasn't been washed since I was in grade eleven.

> E *sees the mirrors. They do a 360° turn pointing to all the mirrors.*

one two three four
I'm surrounded by myself

> *They walk up to the mirror with the towel around them like a cape.*
>
> *They puff their chest out.*
>
> *They play around with taking their shirt off but don't.*
>
> *Each time they are about to they start going off on a tangent.*

hey you know Aunty says the Victorian mob got mirrors and scissors for Country. Batman treaty. Two hundred handkerchiefs, one hundred

pounds of flour, one hundred knives, fifty scissors, forty blankets, thirty axes, thirty mirrors, and six shirts.
Yeah, shit.

> *They play around with taking their shirt off but don't. Look deeply into the mirror.*

I wonder what it would be like to see yourself
for the first time
in the mirror

your reflection:
is it different to seeing yourself
on the water's edge
softened by ripples

is it different to …
do you need to have an image of yourself
to know yourself

> E *does a 360° turn again.*

> E *points.*

is that really me?
or a trick, eh?
are you real?

> E *turns to their side, pulls their shirt up halfway, revealing a bruise on their back.*

> *They finger the bruise in the mirror.*

shhh

> *They turn, see that* SAMENA *has come in and is watching at the door.*

Oh shit.

> *They quickly pull their shirt back down.*

> *They put the towel around them.*

SAMENA: Sorry. Didn't mean to give you a fright! Someone said one of the showers wasn't working … I'll come back …

PART ONE

SAMENA *exits, sneaking another look, playing with her hair but* E *doesn't notice, and when* SAMENA *opens the door another gaggle of women come in and* E *is suddenly crowded for space once more.*

Just when I thought I was alone.
Another lot of bishes come in.
Hey, watch out …
What do I have to do to get some 'me time' in a public pool changing room?

E *slides their body down the mirror until they are squatting.*

SCENE 4: CHANGE

The changing room is empty once again
E *stands up*
puts their towel down.
kicks off their shoes.

All by myself

In front of the mirror
E *looks deeply.*
E *pulls at their t-shirt and tracksuit pants.*

take it off
take it off but also take
off another layer underneath
peel away the expectations
get closer to my truth

E *changes quickly.*

Transforms.

Armoured in a blakfella swimsuit and footy shorts
E *sticks their tongue out at their reflection.*

This is me.

The mirror multiplies their image.

I go back and back and back and back.
I'm not by myself.
I'm surrounded by myself.

SCENE 5: POWDER

Goggles, cap, towel and thongs are spread out in front of E.
They point to a sign on the wall.

all these pool rules you know
no talcum powder in the change rooms
shower before you enter the pool
dry off before you come back

no hairpins, jewellery or glasses
no running, dunking or diving

wasn't too long ago
if you were 'quarter caste'
'half caste' or 'full-blood'
they wouldn't let you swim

I'm thinking I might break a few rules in this joint

It runs deep
the river poisoning
round them up
shoot them down

when they took the water
they stole our way of life
currency and health

on our skin
and our Country
is a battleground

covered up
by something called …
> They clap their hands with powder.

Whiteness
> E *creates plumes of gunpowder*
> *all over the bench and floors of the change room.*

SCENE 6: DANCE

E *gathers their belongings, steps outside into the pool area.*
It's chockers. Sensory overload.
E *chickens out, returns to the change room.*
SAMENA *comes in with a 'Beware Slippery Surface' sign and mop.*
They bump into each other.

E *and* SAMENA: Sorry!

> SAMENA *mops up the talcum powder on the floor, humming.*
>
> E *rushes into a stall, locks the door.*

Don't drive away, Aunty
I've changed my mind
I want to go back home.

> SAMENA *bops along to 'Don't You Worry' by Electric Fields through headphones.*
>
> *The music coaxes* E *out of the stall.*
>
> *It pumps them up.*
>
> *A war dance.*
>
> *They are in the mood to do their own song and dance,*
> *reclaim their body.*

shake it
break it
I'ma make it look sexxxy

make it look sexxxy
make it look sexxxy

tight goggles
make it look sexxxy
fluro green cap
make it look sexxxy
footy shorts
make it look sexxxy
Aunty's floral PJs?
make it look sexxxy
no filter?
make it look sexxxy
pushing five K
make it look sexxxy
crawl, breast, back, butterfly
make it look sexxxy
pit hair
make it look sexxxy
hectic period
make it look sexxxy
crying loud AF
make it look sexxxy
can't go home
make it look sexxxy
pissed myself
make it look sexxxy
lap myself
I'm gonna be sexy

They open the door and dance out into the pool area.

PART TWO: POOL

SCENE 7: SHOW

The pool area is busy and bright.
A giant beach ball.
A lifeguard chair.
A counter with a freezer.
SAMENA *makes announcements from here. Sucking on an iceblock.*

SAMENA: Forgot your goggles, swim cap or sunscreen? No sweat. Come see me at the counter. It's warming up out there. Remember there's hydrating stations in every corner. Have fun and be safe. Please consider others when entering and exiting the pool. We have all eight lanes open today.

    E *gestures to the starting blocks. They light up one by one.*

Lane one and two is for the therapy sessions,
the pool runners, the easy-going, doggy paddlers.
Some of us come here because we are injured and need healing.
Some of us seek healing of another kind.

Lane seven and eight is for the gasbagging, the muck arounds
floating, boating, bopping, hopping
aqua Zumba, fit swim, aerobics
Some of us come here to meet our social needs.
Like a neighbourhood
We find kin in others who swim.

Lane three and four is for the medium lappers
the quick flowing flappers
Perhaps this is where we go
when we overestimate our abilities.
Or we've got a new pair of flippers
that shave time off our laps.

Either way, in this lane,
the one thing you need to know
is the ankle tap, unspoken pool code.
If you feel fingers brushing your ankle
don't stress
it is someone respectfully letting you know
they are overtaking you.

Lane five and six is for the fast fast fast
experienced swimmers need only apply.
we have been in swim squad from day dot.
Our bodies are toned from ten thousand hours
of early starts and extended sessions in the gym.
You may stop and admire our style
so beautiful to watch
you'll wonder if what you've been doing is swimming at all.
I've been told my compulsions are unhealthy
I've had swimmer's ear, swimmer's eye, not to mention
swimmer's hair.
I think in laps, with a ticking clock inside my brain.
If you can't keep the pace step out of the race.

>	E *makes a beeline for lane five.*

>	*They move along the narrow strip beside the pool.*

Squad Boys.
Always in a pack.
Waxed chests and half tights.
Flexing and stretching after their swim
Shoulders back, pecs bouncing
Biceps popping

>	E *adopts a masc pose, having a flex-off with the squad boys.*

Hey, how you going, boys?
Great day for it.

>	*The swim squad boys move past* E.

Speedo Man. There's always one in every public pool.
Tony Abbott vibes.

Stares at your body in a gross way.
Keeps adjusting his budgie smugglers and slapping his thighs.
Hey, Speedo Man, take a photo—it lasts longer!

He loses that smirk real quick.
He's revving for lane five as well
But that's my lane.
I glare at him.
Daggers.
Like how Aunty taught me.
'Stare Indigenously' she says
He snarls.
Spits.
Looks like he's gonna say some sort of fucken comment
I'm coming up with comebacks
before I'm assaulted
like a traumatised dog
teeth out
fuck off
you Ugly Occa Sunburnt Piece of Shit!
I snarl louder
He snarls back
I hold my ground
He elbows
I push
Splash!
He surfaces
gasping for air in the middle of lane eight with the old gurls.
They look at him like 'get the fuck out of our lane, Speedo Man'

    E *runs to claim lane five.*

Lane five. It's all mine.
Nothing's gonna hide my queerness
or my pride
Lane five is where it's at
you can keep watching

    AUNTY *enters.*

AUNTY: Yooo-hoo!
E: Hi Aunty!

SCENE 8: SWIM

E *adjusts their googles above lane five, ready to jump in.*

AUNTY *Lifeguard holds a plastic baby doll*
in a small paddle pool filled with water.
AUNTY *teaches the doll to swim,*
murmuring in language.

AUNTY: Ganngaleh wunga gawal?
E: Aunty says swim
so I float
the echoes haunting me, taunting me

Aunty says 'it's good to move your body right now'
she drags me here kicking and screaming
I'm all good to stay in bed on my phone playing Fruit Ninja eh

Aunty says 'take you out to water on the weekend
to that special spot'

Aunty says lingo
something this something that
'what? You don't know what I mean?
this is important, E.
It's what Nana used to say
You don't remember?'

Aunty says swim
so I float

Aunty says
'never underestimate the ocean'
she pulls me out of a rip when I'm seven

I cling tightly to her chest
I'm so scared
when we reach the shore
she slap me so hard
I cough up the sea I've swallowed
take a deep grateful breath
gawd, I am so embarrassed
my cousin fuckin teases me for weeks

Aunty says swim
so I float

Aunty says
'try going under the wave'
when I'm eight
'duck dive
Ready: three, two ...'
Shit, close my eyes, hold my breath, here we go
'one!'

missed it!
go late
into the belly of the wave
roll around like a footy sock in a cycle
upside down
wait until the wave brings me to shore
coughing and splattering my guts out
and bleeding salt from my ears
Aunty's made it
Her strong back to the shore, her calm head upright.
At one with the ocean.
Next time, I'll be there too

Aunty says
'If you get scared
Call out to Country
Tell em who you are'

Aunty says
'If you get tired
Lie on your back
And let the water carry you'

Aunty says
if I was like straight, like 'straighty-one-eighty'
she wouldn't love me
cos I wouldn't be me
that people like me
have always been in our family
and I shouldn't listen to anything my Uncle says, that's a general rule
Aunty was happy for me to find love
in any shape or form
be with any chick in the world
'yeah, black, white or brindle, love'
but …

Aunty can smell dead fish from the other side of the mountain.

fuck—them lying in the river there
when the water's green

Aunty says
'whenever you feel that tight ball in your chest
just keep breathing'

Aunty says
'touch the water in your belly
feel your power'

Aunty says swim
so I float

Aunty says float
so I …

      E *looks down at the water. Is about to jump but stops.*

SCENE 9: CRAWL

AUNTY *Lifeguard takes out of a box of* E*'s medals and trophies from years past.*
She cleans them and lines them up in a row.
She holds up E*'s squad jacket with WILLIAMS on the back and waves it in the air.*
E *is a bit shamejob by the attention.*

AUNTY: Go bub!
    You can do it!
    I clap so much for ya my palms are red
    I clench so much for ya I get a sore jaw
    I squeal so much for ya I lose my voice
    I sweat so much for ya I lose half a kilo
    I flush so much for ya I almost pass out
    Aww deadly.
    You remind me of your Kumi
    Standing tall and strong
    We love you!

    E *does a few practice strokes with their arms.*

Hey did you know
The Australian Crawl, or Freestyle
Actually came from a Solomon Islander
Alich Wickman
He moved to Sydney when he was seven
Loved being in the water
Diving, bodysurfing, swimming
Spotted in the sea baths on Bronte Beach
by an Australian coach:
'look—that kid's crawling!'
the white mob were amazed by
This short fast arm action
with the head
going from side by side

So they called it the 'Australian Crawl'
adopted into an Olympic machine
a swimming stroke
that runs on white bodies and lycra
Strayla's big hands ready to toy-claw their way
to everything and anything
ready to tongue-kiss their way in

    E *looks down at the pool.*

all the things I learnt at swim school
'breathe at every stroke
keep your legs close
keep breathing
spread your hands'

here we go

SCENE 10: DIVE

E *dives*
into the pool.

SCENE 11: UNDERWATER

E *is underwater*
the sounds of the above world swallowed.
Their breath is bubbles.

I love this sound
What is it?
Gwong?
Gwong, is it?

Water sound
like a tunnel
the rhythm
of my bubbles

everything's monocolour
I can barely see

I'm cold!
but warm
like this chlorine
is sand
like this water
is love

like going back to the beginning
like a womb
a story place
down
deep

in the rivers at home
I can't always see the bottom
Or the top
I feel small
In the vastness of water
I trust the spirits will bring me back
Float me up to the top
for as long as my breath lasts

Gwong
Water

I just feel like playin!

flingin off the swing
into the river
with my cousins
again and again

going to the Heads

bodysurfin in the swell
again and again

divin deep to see what's down the bottom
again and again

if this is another world
I can be another form

>E *opens their hands as they plummet through the water.*

I bring up a star.
I sweep up pebbles.
I catch a fish that jolts in my hands
and I let it go.

I'm a dolphin
spinning my nose through the sea
try and catch me if you can!

>*They do a handstand.*
>*Come up to the surface.*
>*And speed off.*

SCENE 12: LAP

E *pushes off the wall with a dolphin kick.*

touch the wall
turn
touch the wall
turn
touch the wall
turn

when do you find your groove?
touch the wall
turn

for me it's the twelfth lap
touch the wall
turn

I've found my focus
touch the wall
turn

the party's started in my body
touch the wall
turn

each lap is a memory
touch the wall
turn

won a few state medals in back
touch the wall
turn

> *At the end of the pool,* E *slips a few medals around their neck.*

Another in the medley
touch the wall
turn

> E *slips another medal around their neck.*

but never in free
touch the wall
turn

> E *slips another medal around their neck.*

all changed when we got a new coach, ex-Olympic star
touch the wall
turn

> COACH *puts more medals around their neck.*

at my school? Couldn't believe it
touch the wall
turn

A training whistles shrills.
'Nice stroke on that last lap, Williams.'
touch the wall
turn

'Beautiful. Elegant!'
touch the wall
turn

'Shaved two seconds on that one. You're a star.'
touch the wall
turn

feel all lit up,
touch the wall
turn

she doesn't talk to anyone else like that.
touch the wall
turn

could it be, she thinks I'm …?
> *Their strokes become exaggerated, awkwardly mechanical.*
> *Almost violent.*
> *As if cutting.*
> E *stops swimming.*
> *Treads water.*

You say I'm elegant.
You—Coach Casey Burrows, two-time two-hundred-metre freestyle Olympic champion say—
I'm elegant!
Wait—this is exactly what you say—
'I can tell there's *so much elegance* in the way you move, in and out of the pool.'
What the fuck? No-one's ever said anything like that to me before!

PART TWO

The others don't like you.
'She tries too hard.'
Leave her alone, she's alright.
'You're her favourite.'
You reckon?

My Aunty doesn't like you either.
Reckons you're a DH.
So whenever I want to talk about you in front of my Aunty,
I replace you with my friend, Mindy.
Mindy has such beautiful golden eyes.
Mindy likes footy too.
Mindy thinks …
'Mindy this, Mindy that.
Will ya shut up about this Mindy girl
—anyone would think she's the bee's knees!'

Every day I'm excited to go to practice.
I want to run there.
I want to see you.
I think I want … And then you say …

'Williams, Let's chat after practice.
I've got some ideas for the meet tomorrow.'

Everyone leaves
You bring a cool box from your car
Pour fancy bubbly water in tall glasses
You slip vodka in yours,
Then mine.
Butterflies.
I say, I'm not old enough.

You say you first drank at nine
Whisky from your father's cabinet.
You lived in a small country town.
Your cousins helped you reach the shelf and down the bottle.

You tell me you first drove at eleven.
Your dad's pick-up truck on the bush track
You lived in a small country town.
There was no-one on the road.

You tell me you first had sex at thirteen
Your PE teacher put his hand up your skirt at the dance
You lived in a small country town.
You said everyone was doing it.

And I'm almost sixteen.
And I haven't kissed anyone.
Not anyone real.
Just my pillow before I go to sleep
And yes, it's sometimes you.
The way you look at me like a burning tree.
How you say my name.
I can't get you out of my head.
You've had this awesome life
and there's so many other things
you could be doing on a Friday night
but you're here with me.

'It will help you sleep better, have a sip.'
What does it taste like?
'Good.'

Yeah—it tastes good on your tongue.
Cause I am smart, I'm still smart, my head's dizzy.
I need to go home now, for the meet tomorrow.
At least let me draw the line.
I will kiss you but I won't stay in your car any longer.
I need to get home to my family, they'll be wondering after me.
Practice finished two hours ago.

I run all the way home and I can't sleep.

PART TWO

And at the meet I come second last in the four hundred.
You yell at me in front of everyone.
My legs are shaking.
Last night, you put your hand here on my chest
And whispered 'you're elegant, you're beautiful, you're special to me, E.'
You held me.

SCENE 13: TURN

E *gets out of the pool. Slumps over the side.*
They dry their arms and legs slowly.

It was me, I wanted it.
I did it.
I snuck out.
I rode my bike to your house.
Climbed the stairs.
Knocked on the door until you answered.
Asked for us to go to your bedroom.

in my belly
a secret smile
lookin at me like I've never been looked at
you turn the lamp towards my body.

'You want me to be your first?'
'You want to come first?'

    A whistle shrills. E *jumps back into the pool.*

'Lift those legs, lift those legs'

touch the wall
turn

'closer, closer, do I need to tie them?'

touch the wall

turn

'Hey come on, come on, faster'

touch the wall
turn

'race-pace!'

touch the wall
turn

'kick kick kick kick kick'

touch the wall
turn

'that's not good enough!'

touch the wall
turn

'look at your black hair all over the pool.'

touch the wall
turn

'who's gonna clean that up?'

touch the wall
turn

'You're not concentrating. Oi! Look at me!'

touch the wall
turn

'What the fuck is wrong with you?'

PART TWO

E *clutches their neck, overweighed by the medals.*
touch the …
A bucket of water is thrown in their face.
They gasp.

I'm not going to leave you,
I'm never going to leave you,
I don't know why you keep saying that.
I don't love anyone more, I promise.
You want me to prove it? How?

I feel love drunk   humiliated   shocked   excited
   this is not happening   weird   scared   shut down
blocked   hopeless   disgusting   fixated   highly anxious
   disturbed   disconnected   outside myself   not myself
an adult   a child   lost in translation   misunderstood   lost

SCENE 14: HIDE

E *pulls out a dripping red dress from the pool and puts it on.*
They wring out a purse full of water. A dead fish falls out.
They look at their reflection in the water as it distorts.

The first bruises look almost familiar.
I pinch them with my fingers and linger in the mirror until I've seen enough.
The next day I take out my long-sleeved T-shirt from my winter shelf.
Tell Aunty I'm sick.

The days blur between practice, study, exams.
Finding more and more excuses.
My friends, I don't see much of them anymore.
My family, they pissing me off.

'If we get caught, just lie,' you say.
We are so careful.
You're good at this.

Good at letting me know where we're going to meet beforehand.
It's like a secret language.
Aunty suspects.
One day I see her in my room
and she's found the birthday card you got me, sweet sixteen.
I can tell she doesn't believe me.
But nothing will stop me from seeing you.

My graduation.
Aunty and I have biggest blue the day before.
She asks if I still want her to come.
And she wants to book places for my cousins as well.
They are sixty dollars a head
and I know she's been saving for them.
But I tell her not to come.
Go to Minjerribah that weekend instead.
I don't need any of those mob to be there.

Graduation.
I'm so excited you will be there.
I've picked out a red dress I'll know you'll like.
And heels.
And this purse.
You've never seen me in a dress before.
But you're talking to the other teachers and you don't even acknowledge me.
And you've been drinking since … I reckon early afternoon.
When I try to talk to you, you say to the group
'here was the one that could have been something.
If she would have cared enough.
Done something with her talent
One of the laziest swimmers I ever coached.'
And I can't believe you are saying this in front of all these people.
And you know for once, I don't believe you.
I don't believe anything you say.

I grab my purse and get out of there,
and I can feel you following me.
You grab my hand as soon as we're outside.
It's over, I say, brushing you off me.
I don't want anything to do with you.
I don't like how you talk to me.
I don't like how you treat me.
I don't like how you hurt me.
It's not love.
The best part of graduating
is that I don't have to see you every day.

You're shocked, that I stood up to you.
And I use that to my advantage.
I run before you can do anything. I run from you.

Hours later, I'm in bed, almost asleep.
My family are all still away,
I'm the only one home.
I hear a noise outside.
I double check the front door is locked.
I don't want you to come in.

You're yelling, slurring.
I don't know why anyone isn't doing anything.
Somehow the door is open.
You push me hard.
My back hits the wall in slow motion.
I have to get up.
Get up quickly
Run to the bathroom
Close the door
You follow me.
I don't have much time.

I ring Aunty.
Crouching by the sink, hiding.

Try to be quiet.
She picks up the phone on the first ring.
She can hear from the tone of my voice,
and all she needs to know is where I am.
I'm calling the coppas now, she says.
And I don't say anything back.
Just silently nod.

SCENE 15: RIP

The pool goes dark.

Touch the wall
Turn
Touch the wall
Turn

> *The ends of the pool are getting further and further.*
>
> E *is tiring.*

Touch the …
Wall
Turn
Touch the …
Wall
Turn
Touch the …
Touch the …

> E *turns in all directions.*
>
> *They do a 360° turn looking for the horizon.*
>
> E *gets caught in a rip*
>
> *They start laughing.*

Naaah, this water baby Murri can't get caught out like this.
Why didn't I see this coming?
Why didn't I see the deeper darker coloured water?
Why didn't I see the ripple surrounded in stillness?
Why didn't I see the sand from the shallows being dragged back?

PART TWO

How did I get tricked?

Aunty says … when you get caught up in a rip you …
What do you do?!
It's like …
Your lips, my neck.
Your teeth, your hands.
Trying to keep my head above water.
My arms fail me.
I'm alive
But it hurts
I'm alive
But it hurts
I can't think, I can't think, I can't think!
My throat is heavy
I can't breathe

Aunty says … when you get caught up in a rip you …
What do you do? I don't remember.
Aunty says
'Ganngaleh wunga gawal?' *Are you listening?*

> *Churning in the rip,* E *can only hear the voice of Coach,*
> *who drowns out* AUNTY*'s voice.*
>
> E *tenses themselves against the growing waves they can't escape.*

I hear her yell at me again
'You haven't taken any responsibility for your role in this, Williams.
I'll tell everyone what you did. You will pay for this.'

Aunty, I know you told me to change my number
I know you told me not to answer my phone
But I'm not strong enough for
What you're asking me to do
I thought my body was stronger than this.
I thought I was stronger than this.

> *They thrash themself violently at the water,*

> *smacking against an unstoppable force.*
>
> *They are hurting themselves.*

Bleach
If I swallow it will it help?
How much
To disappear?

Come back, Aunty.
You have to come back.
Help me.
Ganngaleh wunga gawal?
Ganngaleh wunga gawal?

> *In open dangerous sea,* E *slips down under a wave, and then another.*
>
> *They are losing.*
>
> *They are drowning.*
>
> E *moves their arms frantically, trying to keep their head above water. They lift up, toes pointed. A giant wave hits. They go down. They kick up.*
>
> *Another big wave hits* E *is knocked right down to the bottom covered in shadow.*

SCENE 16: DUNK

E *is sitting on the bottom of the ocean.*

Down deep
at the bottom
I feel the breath
Leave my body
It is just me
And this weight
holds me down
I don't care if I sink
or swim

> *They lose consciousness, not moving.*
>
> *A torch shines in their face.*
>
> BULLIMAN *interrogates* E.

BULLIMAN: Do you identify as Aboriginal and/or Torres Strait Islander?
E: Aboriginal.
BULLIMAN: Does the respondent identify as Aboriginal and/or Torres Strait Islander?
E: Neither.
BULLIMAN: Do you need legal advice? Is the person who needs protecting under eighteen?
E: No.
BULLIMAN: Are you applying for an application for protection for yourself or on the behalf of someone else?
E: I am applying for myself.
BULLIMAN: Are you in danger right now? Is your web use private? Who needs protection? Given name?
E: E
BULLIMAN: Family name?
E: Williams.
BULLIMAN: Date of birth.
E: Twentieth …
BULLIMAN: Gender.

E: —

BULLIMAN: Who do you need protection from? Given name. Family name. Date of birth. Gender. What is the relationship with the respondent?

E: We have … had … an intimate personal relationship.

BULLIMAN: Reasons why protection is needed.

E: The respondent's behaviour.

BULLIMAN: What kind of behaviour has the respondent shown? How many incidents do you want to describe? One. More than one.

E: One. More than one.

BULLIMAN: When did this happen?

E: Fifteenth November. Eleven p.m.

BULLIMAN: Where did this happen?

E: My current address.

BULLIMAN: What did this respondent do? How did this make you feel? Did anyone witness this?

E: Nobody.

BULLIMAN: Physical threats or harm with objects. Examples: cricket bat, knife, broom, phone.

E: Hate in her eyes.

—

Blood in my mouth. Too many bruises. Feeling shame. Like it's my fault.

BULLIMAN: Remove the respondent from specific premises.

E: Yes/No.

BULLIMAN: Prohibit the respondent from approaching or entering other premises.

E: Yes/ No.

BULLIMAN: Prohibit the respondent from approaching you. Such as shopping centres or events.

E: Yes/ No.

BULLIMAN: Prohibit the respondent from contacting and/or stalking you.

E: Yes.

BULLIMAN: Do you want the respondent to stop publishing anything about you online?

E: Yes.

BULLIMAN: Do you want the respondent to stop trying to find you, including where you live,
E: Yes.
BULLIMAN: or asking someone else to find you?
E: Yes.
BULLIMAN: Do you want the respondent to return your personal property or do you want to be able to collect your personal property?
E: Yes.
BULLIMAN: Do you require protection more urgently?
E: YES.

> *The YES rises them up and they leave the dress behind.*

SCENE 17: GASP

E reaches the surface of the water, breaks through
and gasps for air.

They are in a very different place from where they started.
In deep sea, away from Country.

E turns 360° in the water looking for shore.

This sea is dead cold.
Like it hasn't been warm for years.
I can't see the shore.
Nothing on the horizon.
I'm already too far gone.

> *E turns 360° again.*

> *Long pause. Loneliness.*

I am alone
Hello?

> *E turns 360° again.*

Are you a ghost or a spirit?
I'm not going back down there.
I don't want to go back down there.

> *E turns 360° again.*

breathe
just breathe
breathe
just breathe
breathe
just breathe
breathe with the water.

> E *turns 360° again.*

> E *notices something in the horizon.*

Hey I'm over here, I'm over here, help!

> E *becomes the white woman long-distance swimmer.*

> *Puts on a nose clip and waterproof medical tape, lathers up with Petroleum Jelly.*

> *They swim around in circles, chant manically in a British accent.*

'I am the first, I am the first, I am the first, I am the first.'

> *They take a big suck of air.*

'I am the first. I am the first.
I am the first.
woman to swim from New Zealand to Australia!'

'I belong to an elite group. I've tamed the beast! I've been preparing for this all my life!'

'I swam through seaweed
I swam through lion's mane jellyfish
I swam through box jellyfish
I swam through bull sharks
I swam through tiger sharks
I swam through blue sharks
I swam through great white sharks
It only takes one animal to be in the wrong place
but nothing will stop me'

> *They gasp.*

'I designed a jellyfish mask to protect my face from the stings
but the thing to work out is—how can you control the opening and still
protect the lips?
So I had an orthodontist build a retainer inside the silicon
so I can force my mouth open as I breathe,
and then quickly—because those little buggers are going to get me—
close it tight, fifty times a minute.'

    They demonstrate opening and closing their mouth.

'All major exhibitions start with imagination
I never let go of the vision, the belief
I find a way to get across
I never give up'

'I swam the Oceans Seven:
The 'Seven Summits' of the ocean
The North Channel—Northern Ireland to Scotland
The English Channel—England to France
The Ka'iwi Channel—Hawaii
The Catalian Channel—California
The Cook Strait—New Zealand
The Tsugaru Strait—Honshu to Hokkaido
The Strait of Gibraltar—Morocco to Spain

I swam through strong currents, freezing waters
Hypothermia, paralysis, minor heart attacks, sea urchins

I swam through sexism
Glass ceilings
Double standards

Just extreme mental strength. I don't crumble. I just keep powering through!

I am what it takes!

I am the first. I am the first. I am the first. I am the first.'

The long-distance swimmer speeds away, leaving E *alone.*

Oh. There she goes. What was that?
She womba one eh?

    The water churns.
    A storm begins.

SCENE 18: RESCUE

The churning intensifies.
Pounding rain. Howling wind.
E *is in a big storm.*
high and rough water.

    The waves batter me.
Gulp
    A wave knocks me
Gasp.
    A plastic bag in the face. Smack.
Gulp.
    Another strong wave.
Gasp.
    Tangled in a net.
Gulp.
    A wave sends me spinning.
Gasp.

        E *clutches their leg.*

Ouch, cramp.
I can't escape the storm
Hot and cold waves mix
It hits
I am swallowed

        They start to panic. They can't move.

Aunty says
whenever you feel that tight ball in your chest
just keep breathing

PART TWO

Aunty says
touch the water in your belly
feel your power

Aunty says ...
Breathe
Just breathe

Breathe
Just breathe

'If you get scared
Call out to Country
Tell em who you are'

Gwong
Jumgan
Nganyi

>   *The storm clouds part.*
>
>   E *swims eagerly towards shore but is pulled down by the current.*

So close
But I'm caught
can't see the bottom
can't touch the bottom
near rocks
can't see

'If you get tired
Lie on your back
And let the water carry you'

Breathe
Just breathe

Tchoorella
Float
The water and me are one
We are a part of each other.

Breathe
Just breathe

> *They flip over onto their back*
> *To let the water carry them.*
> *Like a pulse.*
> *Silence.*
> *They let themselves go.*

AUNTY: [*in distance*] COOO-EEE

> E *turns to where the sound is.*
> *Smoke rises in the sky.*

fire
a signal
I see the shore.

> AUNTY *chucks a floatie.*
> E *catches it and kicks all the way to shore, to the glowing fire.*

SCENE 19: FIRE

High up on the beach,
E *and* AUNTY *set up camp*
stoking the fire and settling in.
drying towels and
boiling water.

E *takes off the medals*
And lines them up on the sand.

E *sets down a cuppa for* AUNTY.

They weave together.
The weaving is like a dance, it holds time.

AUNTY: Keep holdin on that needle, E.
you'll get there.
E: soz, Aunt I don't think I'm good at this
too delicate, too fiddly
I got man-hands, see
they were made for cutting through water!
catching a footy! One-hand!
AUNTY: Hey, just look at this, see.
Under, over.
Under, over
See the gap

We're pulling that through
About halfway
that becomes another row
fills in that gap
And that helps to grow the weave.

E: I can't get the hang of this.
AUNTY: let your mind rest
If you do it funny, keep going
If you make a mistake, don't worry
Baskets have their own minds sometimes
I pick this dhilla over there
Soak it in the river
Clean it
Dry it out
Don't dye it
Weave in feathers, hair
And yarns
Our weave is our strength
Our connection
We almost lost this weaving
It was sleeping

  But we are waking it up
  And we gotta be loud
E: water is my weaving

  E walks over to the sea.

AUNTY: when the tide is coming in
  this beach
  is a time warp
E: is this another one of your lessons, Aunty?
AUNTY: We faced three waves here
  when the sand is like this
  we can feel the past
  with our jinnungs
  vibrating through us
  whispering in our binnungs

  our ancestors tell us to run
  the big white wave comes
  not just one wave, two, and then three
  the first knocks us off our feet
  and sets us drifting
  the second carries us across sharp rocks
  where we snap
  and the third
  the third lives in us

  E sees something on the horizon.

E: What is that?

  E becomes the long-distance swimmer.

'I am the first, I am the first, I am the first, I am the first.'
AUNTY: Who is that? What is she doing?
E: 'I've been swimming for over twenty-eight hours. I can't feel my legs. Chunks of my tongue are falling out. I've got this. Got to keep going.

  The long-distance swimmer slows down. The pace is tragic but determined.

'I am the first, I am the first, I am the first, I am the first.'

AUNTY: Who does she reckon she is?
E: She's the first.
A: *She's* the first?
E: She's the first. She womba one, hey Aunt?

'I am the first, I am the first, I am the first, I am the first.'

> E *and* AUNTY *watch the long-distance swimmer go past.*

E *and* AUNTY: [*together real slow*] Womba one

> AUNTY *takes the medals* E *left behind*
> *before the tide washes them away.*
> *She puts them in her basket*

AUNTY: The sun is low. It's getting late
> Time to follow our tracks. Go home. Back to the river.
>
> E *and* AUNTY *go back to the fire.*
>
> *The glow lights their steps along the river.*

> This beautiful river
> curls round the bend
> mob there on the banks fishing
> laughing
> scrub
> thin grey trunks of trees catch light
> geese, more laughter
>
> Dugulumba

E: this river
AUNTY: Bugeram
E: is sacred

> *With her finger,* AUNTY *traces down the vein on* E*'s arm.*
>
> AUNTY *touches her heart.*

AUNTY: in our language
> river is blood
> river is love
> goomera and goomera

> E *touches their vein and* AUNTY*'s heart too.*
>
> *At the river mouth,* AUNTY *puts her hat on and sets her lilo down.*
>
> E *stops at the water's edge.*
>
> Go'on!
>
> E *jumps in.*

Freshwater
Like silk on my skin
bit of river goes up my nose
down my throat
I taste chlorine
and I see those lanes again
walls
other swimmers
concrete
buildings
but it doesn't matter
I'm in water

> *A whistle shrills.*
>
> AUNTY *passes* E *their towel, swimming cap and goggles.*

SCENE 20: RACE

A Barkaa track plays through the speakers.

Back at the pool, AUNTY *sits in the stands with her basket weaving, watching* E.

E *is swimming fast.*
They get into a great rhythm, confident stroke.

touch
turn
touch
turn
touch
turn

touch
turn
touch
turn
touch
turn

getting to my last k
feeling good
when splashes enter my lane
a hand hits my leg
rude!
I hear a gross pant beside me
Getting in front
It's Speedo Man

Fucken bring it!
AUNTY: Go, bub!
> *They decide to race, commentating at the same time.*
>
> AUNTY *cheers* E *on with black, red and yellow streamers.*

Williams in lane five in the lime green cap.
Speedo Man in lane four in the red cap
and the offensive Tony Abbott budgie smugglers
Williams
Speedo Man
Williams has the lead
Speedo Man in lane four just losing a bit more ground now.
Williams.
Then Speedo Man as they hit the turn.
coming up now making ground.
But Williams is swimming an excellent race.
They are in such great form, the twenty-year-old.
They are definitely back
And they are definitely Blak
The crowd goes wild.

AUNTY: You got this, darling.
Wait—we've had a late addition to this race
Coming up out of nowhere in lane six
'I am the first, I am the first, I am the first, I am the first.'
It's Womba Woman!
'I am the first, I am the first, I am the first, I am the first.'
Those flippers are leaping her forward
And she's caught up to the others
Speedo Man hits the turn strong
So does Williams
Williams is just inching in front
It's millimetres
Womba Woman is not giving up her position easily
She's got some movement there
She's really starting to challenge
'I am the first, I am the first, I am the first, I am the first.'
'I am the first, I am the first, I am the first, I am the first.'
'I am the …Ouch!'
Oh my goodness
Have you ever seen this before?
Womba Woman has been stung by an octopus!
Anaphylaxis! Does anyone have an EpiPen?
Well we do hope she will be okay
The medical team are doing their work off the side of the pool
Lane five and Lane four are battling it out
There's so much on the line
Williams' technique is incredible
They don't fight the water
They move with it
Looking smooth at the halfway mark
They lead Budgie Smugglers by nearly a body length
Hey lookout it's ScoMo
In his Hawaiian shirt
And K Rudd
What's he doing
He's here to say sorry
Noel Pearson's backstroking

Jacinta Price is bombing in!
Andrew Bolt is trying to grab
Williams' ankles
AUNTY: Get off!
Don't worry, Aunty's sorting him out!
With so many competitors
Williams is losing some momentum here
Can they hang on?
Speedo Man is catching up
Taking water away from the leader
Speedo Man has overtaken
he looks really happy
It's not looking good for Williams

> *At the end of the pool* AUNTY *passes* E *a bowl of roo stew which they scoff.*

Speedo Man hits the turn well
He is looking like he can steal a win here
But E has something in the belly
A boost
A second wind?
Williams is looking looser
They got more spring in those arms
Legs are powering
That roo stew must've really helped
Can I get the recipe, Aunty?
Long reach with the stroke
Relaxed hands
And that kick is working nicely
Speedo Man is not giving up his lead
This race is going down to the wire.
This last turn will be important
Lane five
Then lane four
Excellent underwater by Williams
They are ahead once more
They are swimming this race in their own way

The kick is like a motor
But Speedo Man is not going away
Williams
Speedo Man
On no, Williams is clutching their side
Stitch?
they'll need a bit extra here.
Aunty's coming over with a cuppa
Strong, black and sweet—just like Aunty!

> AUNTY *passes* E *a cuppa which they gulp down.*

Wow! Williams is on world record pace now.
They put their head under the water and surge.

Williams	Budgie Smugglers
Williams	Budgie Smugglers
Williams	Williams
Williams	Williams!

They got it.
And they've broken the world record too.
What a remarkable story.

> E *takes a triumphant touch of the block,*
>
> *Punching their fist. Waving to* AUNTY.
>
> *They lift themself up, back on dry land.*
>
> *They slip their cap and googles off.*
>
> *Pretend to be interviewed by Channel 9.*
>
> *Put on a gammin athlete voice.*
>
> *Hands on hips, sucking in some big breaths.*

Cheers, mate.	Gulp
One hundred percent, yeah.	Gulp
Had to go for it.	Gulp
Gave it all for my mob!	Gulp
Couldn't have done it without them.	Gulp
Especially my Aunty	Gulp
The last cup of tea on the fifteenth	Gulp
It really got me over the line!	

PART TWO

'Black & Deadly' by The Last Kinection plays through the speakers.

AUNTY *comes over for presentation ceremony.*

E *stands on the gold medal block.*

AUNTY *puts the dilly bag she's been weaving around* E*'s neck.*

Thanks, Aunty.
Beautiful.
Whatcha reckon?
My best trophy yet.

They hug and kiss.

E *makes a speech*

I used to think winning was everything
But winning is thin
winning is temporary
ultra-white competition doesn't do it for me
cos what do I lose
when I push water to its limits?

the whitefella way—winning at all costs
Winning against Country
Tearing up the banks of the river with speedboats
Killing the mangroves—the lifeforce
Making a billion-dollar harbour
Mining our springs for minerals
Killing Wardam because they want to claim the ocean
And make it theirs
No—that's not our way

What is more important than winning?
Aunty taught me
Connection
Feeling
Country
Respect
Knowledge

I dedicate this swim to
Uncle Alick Wickman
The Solomon Islander swimmer
The holder of the stroke I just swam
It's not the *Australian* Crawl
Australia stole it.
Like they steal everything.
This is yours, Uncle Alick
It's about time we returned the credit to you

This is for the mob out there
This is for all of us
Don't let anyone else define you
Don't give up
Know you belong

And this is for me
Cos I just remembered
I am really deadly

PART THREE: TRANSFORMATION ROOM

SCENE 21: SHOWER

Back in the unpopulated changeroom, E *makes a beeline for a shower.*
They turn the tap on all the way.
A gush of water spurts out.
They put their head under the water.

after the storm
the rain
the tropics
open up
soak my skin
cleanses me new

this shower's a waterfall
freshwater washing off everything
I don't need

> *They sigh deeply, blowing the snot out of their nose under the water.*

freshwater washing off the ache
in my body
tea tree seeping in
lemon myrtle
lemon grass
healing
breathing

I feel fresh
Smooth
Supple
Soft
Lux

Slippery
Gliding
Sliding

this water
doesn't stop falling
flowing
feeding
moving
giving

>*They massage their hair and scrub their skin.*

so good to feel clean
sooo good—

>*On an external timer, the shower stops.*
>
>E *opens their hands to water that doesn't come.*

aww nah … already? I was just getting started.

>*Groaning, they reach for their towel and put their face in it.*

SCENE 22: DRESS

E *walks confidently around the change room in their binder and boyshorts.*

They dry themselves off.

Spot their reflection in the central mirror and walk up to take a closer look.

They talk to themselves quietly.

you race against guilt, shame
and it feels like it's never going to end

It's okay, babe, it's alrite.
You good.
It's over.
You got this.

I'm buoyant as, bish.
My fam—they're my biggest strength.
I'm fluid as fuck.

Aunty says
this gwong
is our belonging

> *They get out zinc lippie and draw in an outline on the mirror*
> *of those big fat Murri lips of theirs*
> *and crack themselves up.*

Aw, bless!

> SAMENA *enters. Electric Fields' 'Gold Energy' plays through*
> *speakers.*
>
> *In front of the mirror,* E *opens their bag,*
> *now a fancy dress box with all sorts of goodies.*

Samena comes in to mop up a spill
sees me in my new flash top and shorties
and my deadly pit hair
my skin feels so smooth
and my hair's all spiked up
I put on this moisturiser someone's left behind
rub it in all over
smells really sweet, like mangoes
thinking of that post work-out snack
banana smoothie
coconut
honey
mango
juicy
rich

> E *takes their time lathering the moisturiser in*
> *really pampering themself*
> E *rubs their way into a dance.*

> *Dancing their way around the change room.*
>
> *The song stops.*
>
> *They put the moisturizer down.*
>
> *They throw clothes out of their bag onto the floor, like jackets, hats, ties.*
>
> *Searching for inspiration.*
>
> E *finds something in the bag they like.*
>
> *They slip a soft button-up shirt*
>
> *around their shoulders*
>
> *and pull on dress pants, leather belt, shoes.*

Samena, eh?
she's put that mop down now
she's only pretending to clean up
she lookin at me.

> *Dressing like someone's watching,*
>
> E *fit on a smart hat on their head.*
>
> *They top off their outfit with Haus of Dizzy earrings*
>
> *that say FUCK THE DATE*
>
> *and puts the dilly bag* AUNTY *made for them around their neck.*
>
> *They do a little spin.*

dapper Blak!
all ready to go NAIDOC Ball
or maybe a date with uhhh …
yeah
she's asking me if I had a good swim
I say it was alrite
lean against the mirror all casual like
ask her if she's uh responsible for the great trax on the speakers
she says yes, that was her, asks me where I got my hat and my shoes
sorta looks at me with that flirty-eye
like she uh skipped lunch

yes!
deadly!

> E *goes up to* SAMENA *and puts one of the earrings in her ear.*
>
> *A mirrorball glistens*
>
> ROMANTIC MUSIC.
>
> *They waltz.*
>
> *A song starts.*
>
> *The room becomes a river*
>
> E *holds* SAMENA*'s hand and guides her with whispers of* AUNTY.

E: Goomera
SAMENA: River
E: Goomera
E *and* SAMENA: Blood.
    Love.

SCENE 23: GUNDALAH

E *and* SAMENA *get into a gundalah*
and paddle out the change room
hear mob in small dug-out canoes, singing,
E *and* SAMENA *greet them, softly tapping the water*
with handcrafted paddles
in unison to the rhythm of the song.

The song carries them down the river.
They paddle and paddle into the horizon
where sun and water meet.

THE END

GRIFFIN THEATRE COMPANY PRESENTS

SWIM

BY ELLEN VAN NEERVEN

10 – 27 JULY 2024 | TRACK 8, CARRIAGEWORKS

GRIFFIN
THEATRE
COMPANY

CAST & CREATIVES

Director Andrea James
Movement Director Kirk Page
Designer Romanie Harper
Lighting Designer Karen Norris
Composer & Sound Designer Brendon Boney
Video Designer Samuel James
Cultural Consultant Aunty Jenny Fraser
Cultural Consultant Lann Levinge
Cultural Consultant Aunty Maria van Neerven
Gender & Inclusivity Consultant Bayley Turner
Stage Manager Isabella Kerdijk
Production Manager Damion Holling
Senior Producer Elinor King
Associate Producer Cassie Hamilton
Associate Producer Paris Mordecai
With Sandy Greenwood, Dani Sib
Workshop Dramaturg Bryan Andy
Workshop Choreographer Yolande Brown
Workshop Performer Hannah Donnelly

SPECIAL THANKS

BlakDance— Merindah Donnelly, Kate Eltham, Tom Pritchard, Olivia Adams
BLEACH* Festival— Rosie Dennis & Claire Carlin
HotHouse Theatre— Karla Conway, Beck Palmer, Tiffany Ward
Queensland Performing Arts Centre— Brad Chatfield & Hannah Scanlon
Yugambeh Museum— Aunty Pat

Abbie Stott / Ali Murphy Oates / Anne & Steve Carlin /
Bee Cruse / Callie Rowbuck / Dalara Williams / Aunty Erica Eurell /
Greg Murphy Scenery / Justine Dillon / Lily Shearer / Liza-Mare Syron /
Miimi & Jiinda / Moreblessing Maturure / Dr Paula Abood / Sally Quade /
Dr Sandy O'Sullivan

PRESENTING PARTNERS

SUPPORTED BY

GOVERNMENT PARTNERS

swim has been assisted by the Australian Government through Creative Australia, its arts funding and advisory body and supported by the Queensland Government through Arts Queensland and by the NSW Government through Create NSW. This project was first developed by Moogahlin Performing Arts through the Yellamundie Festival 2019. Script development continued in 2020 by Moogahlin Performing Arts, with the support of the Department of Theatre and Performance Studies at the University of Sydney. Creative developments have received generous support from Malcolm Robertson Foundation, Robert Dick and Erin Shiel and Home of the Arts (HOTA). swim has been developed with support from BlakDance and continued support from Queensland Performing Arts Centre.

Elinor King's role as Senior Producer and **Paris Mordecai**'s role as Associate Producer are generously supported by **Shane & Cathryn Brennan**.

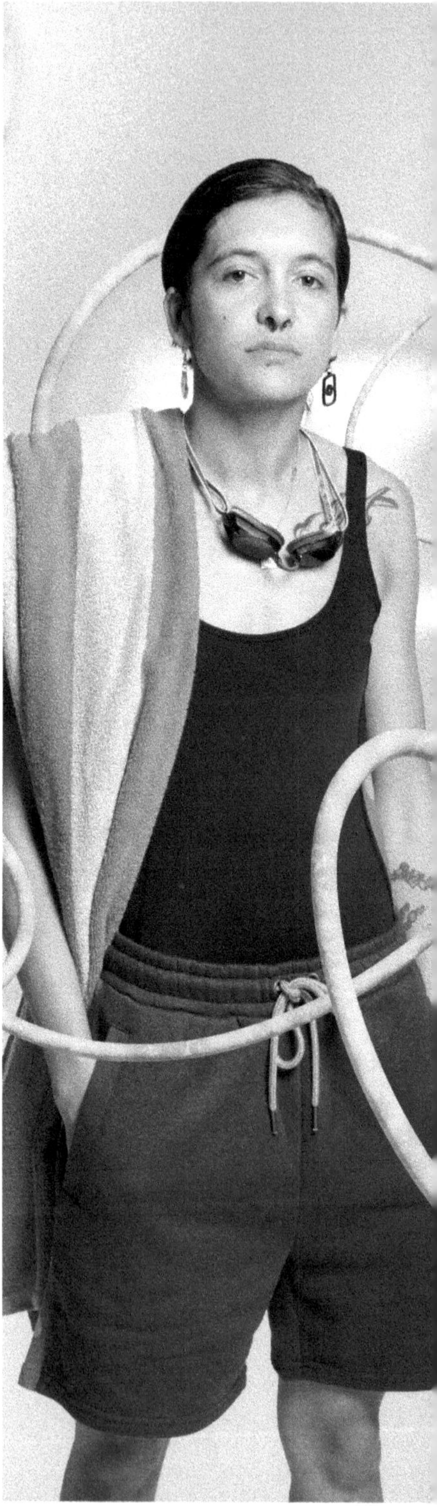

PLAYWRIGHT'S NOTE

Jingeri Jimbelung. It is my cultural obligation to acknowledge the lands, skies and waterways this work has taken shape on, and pay my deepest respect to the traditional owners and recognising that sovereignty was never ceded.

Like many of my ideas, this work came from being with my body in water. *swim* had its very early beginnings while I was on a residency at Campbelltown Arts Centre on Dharawal Land in 2017. Experiencing writer's block, I took solace in the local pool. From there, the work was selected for Moogahlin Performing Arts' Yellamundie Festival in 2019 where I first worked with director **Andrea James**.

swim is a commentary on Australian swimming, the sovereignty of water and the strength of culture and family in keeping us safe. When we examine the sites of surf beaches and public swimming pools on stolen land—we can question who feels safe here. To Aboriginal and Torres Strait Islander people, water is life—yet since colonisation, a legacy of aqua nullius has set to erase the reciprocal connections between people and waterways, with extreme consequences, such as the disaster in the Murray-Darling Basin. The Crown has the powers to control the flow and use of water in almost all states and territories in so-called Australia. As much as *swim* speaks on a national level, I took a lot of inspiration from how these complexities play out in the specific locale of Yugambeh Country. We had the pleasure to spend time as a creative team there on two separate occasions.

When I swim, I feel well, connected and proud. Yet swimming also has a complex legacy of exclusion and shame. I set out to write about what swimming means, on a personal and political level. The story we tell is one that honours and celebrates SBLGBTIQA+ people—especially our Blak siblings. I felt it important to let E's voice be heard at a time where transphobia and queerphobia has been simmering fuelled by hostile coverage by the right-wing press. As Blak queer and trans folk, we feel an intense responsibility to honour and support both our Elders and the younger generation.

I am grateful to the artists involved in each development for first holding space for the story and all supporters. Thanks so much to everyone from Griffin Theatre Company. It is a privilege to have my first work for the stage with a theatre company that champions exciting and vital new work. I also thank the entire creative team and the cast—the 'swim team'. Special thanks to director Andrea James who kept the interest and passion in the project alive since Yellamundie. To my family of blood and water—bugalwan—I am so grateful.

EvN
(they/them/theirs)
Mununjali Yugambeh writer

DIRECTOR'S NOTE

I first had the privilege of working on **Ellen van Neerven**'s *swim* when it was presented as a reading at Moogahlin Performing Arts' Yellamundie Festival in 2019. A huge admirer of Ellen's work, I was (and still am) floored by Ellen's culturally and politically connected writing that cuts to the chase in the most resonant way. Ellen is ahead of their time and we are playing catch up. Ellen is also wickedly funny.

From the get go, Ellen's play *swim* made an impression. For months and years after the reading at Yellamundie, people were asking me about "that play". Ellen and I kept yarning and we eventually found a safe and good home to bring the play to stage readiness. As the play gently evolved, the story and characters blossomed into fullness.

Little did I know, Ellen was quietly brewing another literary work—the ambitiously poetic and personal memoir *Personal Score* that is an exploration of Identity Sport and Politics from a Blak Gender Queer lens. In many ways, *swim* is the performance arm of Ellen's deeper thinking around sport, competition and gender fluidity on and in sovereign lands and waters.

Who can forget those vivid images at the Moree swimming pool in 1965 on Gamilaraay land—and the bigoted backlash that took place—when Charlie Perkins dared to lead a group of young Blak kids as they dive bombed their way into a basic human right. The local pool—that most Australians enjoy and take for granted—can be a very dangerous place if you're Blak; and that danger is multiplied ten-fold when you're Blak and Gender Queer.

Ellen's play *swim* offers an antidote to the colonial clash of one of Australia's most revered sites—the municipal swimming pool. Ellen's exquisite poetry and fluid storytelling challenges this colonial battleground through an ultimate celebration of Blak Gender Queer resilience and the most sacred of elements on Country—water.

Connecting to and experiencing Yugambeh lands and waters has been an absolutely essential part of the project. Thank you to **Aunty Maria van Neerven, Aunty Jenny Fraser** and **Lann Levinge** who welcomed and guided us onto Country with great generosity and wisdom.

I also give credit to our performers, **Dani Sib** and **Sandy Greenwood**. Thank you for bringing your realness, courage and vulnerability to your roles to honor Ellen's story. For them, this isn't an act—it's a part of their everyday.

Ellen asks us to immerse ourselves fully into their world—to see and recognize danger when it occurs and to understand that bigotry, transphobia and hatred threatens lives (physically and spiritually) and to do something about it. We are asked to recognize our power and privilege and to give ground.

swim shows us that love, family and cultural connection is the elixir of life.

swim is a gift to Australia. A healing. A bath.

Andrea James
Director

BIOGRAPHIES

ELLEN VAN NEERVEN
PLAYWRIGHT, (THEY / THEM)

Ellen van Neerven is an award-winning writer of Mununjali Yugambeh and Dutch heritage. They have authored two poetry collections, *Throat* and *Comfort Food*, one work of fiction, *Heat and Light*, and a memoir called *Personal Score*. *Throat* won three categories at the 2021 NSW Premiers Literary Awards including Book of the Year, the Kenneth Slessor Prize and the Multicultural Award.

ANDREA JAMES
DIRECTOR, (SHE / HER)

Andrea is a Yorta Yorta/Gunaikurnai award-winning theatremaker and Associate Artistic Director of Griffin Theatre Company. Andrea's directing credits for Griffin include *Ghosting the Party* by Melissa Bubnic and *Jailbaby* by Suzie Miller. As Playwright and Director, Andrea has written and directed productions including: for Belvoir St Theatre and Geelong Performing Arts Centre: *Winyanboga Yurringa*; for Melbourne Workers Theatre with Playbox Theatre Company: *Yanagai! Yanagai!*, which went on to tour internationally to the UK; for Moogahlin Performing Arts: *Winyanboga Yurringa*; and for Performing Lines: *Sunshine Super Girl*, which then had an extensive national tour. Andrea's co-writing credits include: for Griffin: *Dogged*, with Catherine Ryan; for Sydney Festival: *Big Name No Blankets*, with Sammy and Anyupa Butcher about the life and times of Aboriginal rock legends *The Warumpi Band*.

KIRK PAGE
MOVEMENT DIRECTOR, (HE / HIM)

Kirk Page is a proud Munanjali artist with patriarchal connections from South East QLD of the Yugambeh nation and ancestral lineage connecting him to Badu Island in the Torres Straits. His matriarchal lineage is connected to Polish and German heritage migrant settlers. Kirk trained at NAISDA Dance College (National Aboriginal and Islander Skills Development Association). Since 1995, he has performed on national mainstages and toured productions internationally. His practice and experience in the arts sector is interdisciplinary – spanning dance, acting, singing, directing, teaching, producing and writing over the past 28 years.
He is currently based on Bundjalung Territories in the Northern Rivers Region of NSW.

BIOGRAPHIES

ROMANIE HARPER
DESIGNER, (SHE / HER)

Romanie Harper is an award-winning Set and Costume Designer based in Naarm/Melbourne. Recent design credits include: for Performing Lines: *Sunshine Super Girl*; for Melbourne Theatre Company: *Girls & Boys* and *The Violent Outburst That Drew Me To You*; for Rising Festival: *8/8/8: WORK*; for Belvoir St Theatre: *The Master and Margarita*, *The Cherry Orchard* and *Packer and Sons*; for Malthouse Theatre: *Nosferatu, K-Box, Australian Realness, Trustees, Good Muslim Boy, Little Emperors* and *Turbine*; for Deep Soulful Sweats: *What Am I Supposed to Do?* and *Equinox*; for Arts House: *Hercules, Die! Die! Die! Old People Die!, We All Know What's Happening* and *Never Trust A Creative City*; for Darebin Speakeasy: *Slip, Conviction, Contest and Moral Panic*; for fortyfivedownstairs: *Runt* and *This Is Eden*; and for Daniel Schlusser Ensemble: *M+M*.

KAREN NORRIS
LIGHTING DESIGNER, (SHE / HER)

Karen Norris is a Lighting Designer for theatre, dance, and installations from Aotearoa of Moriori Maori decent.

In Australia, Karen's recent theatre credits include: for Adelaide Festival: *Action Star*; for ATYP: *Sugarland*; for Belvoir St Theatre: *Barbara and the Camp Dogs*; for Carriageworks: *Sleeplessness*; for Ensemble Theatre: *The Appleton Ladies Potato Race* and *The Last Five Years*; for Moogahlin Performing Arts: *Broken Glass, Cutter & Coota, The Last Shot, Rainbows End, The Weekend* and *Winyanboga Yurringa*; for National Theatre of Parramatta: *Choir Boy*; for Performing Lines: *Sunshine Super Girl* and *TWO*; for Rising Festival: *Set Piece*; for Sydney Festival: 宿 *(Stay)*; for Sydney Theatre Company: *The Visitors*; for Urban Theatre Projects: *Blak Box* and *M'ap Boulé*.

Karen's Australian and international dance credits include: for Atamira Dance Company NZ: *KOTAHI*; for Australian Ballet: *Dance X*; for Bangarra Dance Theatre: *The Dreaming, Dance Clan 202, Horizon, LORE, Skin, Terrain*, and *Yuldea*; for BlakDance and Karul Projects: *Silence*; for Jasmin Sheppard: *The Complications of Lyrebirds*; for Liz Lea Dance: *The Point* and *Red*; for Martin del Amo: *Champions* and *Songs Not To Dance To*; for Narelle Benjamin: *CELLA Germany* and *Hiding in Plain Sight*; for NAISDA: *Francis Rings*; for Rhiannon Newton: *Explicit Contents*; for Sue Healey: *On View*; for Vicki Van Hout: *plenty serious TALK TALK*.

BIOGRAPHIES

BRENDON BONEY
COMPOSER & SOUND DESIGNER, (HE / HIM)

Brendon Boney is a Wiradjuri/Gamilaroi man who grew up in Wagga Wagga, New South Wales and is now based on Darkinjung Country in Ettalong Beach on the Central Coast of New South Wales. Brendon's work as Sound Designer & Composer includes: for Bangarra Dance Theatre: *Horizon: The Light Inside* and *Kulka, Dance Clan*; for Belvoir St Theatre: *At What Cost?*, *Lose to Win*, *Winyanboga Yurringa*; for Ensemble Theatre: *A Letter for Molly*; for National Theatre of Parramatta/Riverside Theatres: *Choir Boy*; and for Sydney Theatre Company: *Fences, A Raisin in the Sun, The Visitors*. Brendon's Design Associate credits include: for Sydney Theatre Company: *The 7 Stages of Grieving* and *The Tempest*. His television music credits include: for ABC1: *Gods of Wheat Street*; for Network 10: *Offspring*; for Seven Network: *Winners & Losers*; and for The Nine Network: *Underbelly Chopper*. As an actor and performer, his recent credits include: for ABC: *At Home Alone Together*; for Adelaide Festival: Stephen Page's *Baleen Moondjan*; for Bangarra Dance Theatre: *Wudjang: Not the Past*; and for Illbijerri Theatre: *Black Ties*. Brendon also provided the lead character Willie's singing voice in the feature film, *Bran Nue Dae* (2009).

Brendon is an established recording and performing artist and an APRA PDA winner. In the past decade, he has toured the world with the act Microwave Jenny. As a producer and songwriter Brendon's work has over a million streams across platforms Spotify and Apple Music.

SAMUEL JAMES
VIDEO DESIGNER, (HE / HIM)

Samuel James is a Filmmaker and Projection Designer living on Gundungarra and Dharug land, Blue Mountains. Over 30 years he has collaborated with performance companies with a focus on dance movement and digital projection. His work is often seen in festivals of various scales in Australia, and he has worked internationally in Europe, Canada, South Korea. He has developed work on international residencies in Norway, Czech Republic, Iceland, Finland, Banff, Calcutta and Berlin. He has been privileged to work with many Indigenous artists and companies taking the opportunity to develop understandings of sovereignty of country and applies this expanding image archive to collaborative works in theatrical, urban and natural environments. His videos incorporate drawings in which superimposed mark making is an unconscious response to spirit of place. He has an MFA from the UNSW School of Art and Design. *shimmerpixel.blogspot.com*

BIOGRAPHIES

BAYLEY TURNER
GENDER & INCLUSIVITY CONSULTANT, (SHE / HER)

Bayley Turner is the founder of Create Consent, consulting with creative production teams on consent-centred creative practices, intimacy coordination, policy and protocol documentation and facilitating bespoke workshops locally and internationally with theatre and film projects. In Australia, she has worked on productions including: for Griffin: *Jailbaby* and *The Lewis Trilogy*; for Apocalypse Theatre: *Cleansed*; for Darlinghurst Theatre Company: *Let the Right One In, Natasha, Pierre & the Great Comet of 1812* and *Overflow*; for fortyfive downstairs: *The Inheritance*; for Melbourne Theatre Company: *The Almighty Sometimes*; and for Theatre Works: *In the Club*. She has also delivered workshops with Malthouse Theatre and various independent companies. Bayley completed her Master's thesis on consent in the creative workplace, conceived and led the organising of Consent Festival (Midsumma 2019), and has presented at various local and international conferences. In 2021, she received a MEAA scholarship to train with IDC Professionals, compounding her training with Intimacy on Set, and is currently the Intimacy Coordinator on the return season of Australian soap *Neighbours*. Bayley is also a writer, performer and theatremaker. *create-consent.com*

BIOGRAPHIES

ISABELLA KERDIJK
STAGE MANAGER, (SHE / HER)

Isabella graduated from the production course at the National Institute of Dramatic Art in 2008. She has worked as a Stage Manager and Assistant Stage Manager on many shows, including: for Griffin: *And No More Shall We Part*, *Blaque Showgirls*, *Green Park*, *Replay*, *Sex Magick*, *The Smallest Hour*, *This Year's Ashes*, *Ugly Mugs*, *Whitefella Yella Tree* and *Wicked Sisters*; for Belvoir St Theatre: *An Enemy of the People*, *The Dog/The Cat*, *The Drover's Wife*, *Every Brilliant Thing*, *FANGIRLS*, *Girl Asleep*, *The Glass Menagerie*, *HIR*, *Jasper Jones*, *Kill the Messenger*, *Mother*, *Mother Courage and Her Children*, *My Name is Jimi*, *Stories I Want to Tell You In Person* (National Tour), *The Sugar House*, *Thyestes* (European Tours) and *Winyanboga Yurringa*; for Sydney Theatre Company: *Blithe Spirit*; for Circus Oz: *Cranked Up*; for Darlinghurst Theatre Company: *Fourplay*, *Ride* and *Silent Night*; for Ensemble Theatre: *Benefactors*, *Boxing Day BBQ*, *Rainman* and *The Ruby Sunrise*; for Legs on the Wall: *Bubble*; for LWAA: *The Mousetrap* (Australia/New Zealand Tours); for Spiegelworld: *Empire*. Isabella has worked as Production Coordinator for Opera Australia's *Carmen* and Production Manager/Stage Manager for A-List Entertainment's *Puppetry of the Penis*. She has also worked on various festivals, including The Garden of Unearthly Delights, Sydney Festival and the Woodford Folk Festival.

DANI SIB
E, (THEY / THEM)

Dani Sib is a proud Baad and Yawuru multidisciplinary artist from the Kimberley in Western Australia. They started playing guitar when they were 8 years old, singing at 12 years old, and now creates music that reflects their experiences of navigating life as a young First Nations person.

In 2018, Dani co-produced and presented *BBQ: Blak, Beautiful and Queer*, a music and performance night celebrating the deadly young queer Aboriginal and Torres Strait Islander folk. They also produced *Jirrmujina Liyan* (*Songs for Spirit*) that same year, through Darebin's AMPLIFY program, presenting a full lineup of First Nations musicians.

Dani made their performance debut as Marijuanna Annie in the *Bran Nue Dae* Musical Tour 2020. Dani is excited to be exploring the world of theatre further in Ellen van Neerven's *swim*.

BIOGRAPHIES

SANDY GREENWOOD
SAMENA, AUNTY, (TWO SPIRIT)

Sandy Greenwood is a Gumbaynggirr, Dunghutti and Bundjalung Traditional Custodian raised (and living) on her ancestral homelands.

Sandy holds a BA in Drama (Honours) from QUT and has trained at The Atlantic Acting School in New York City and The Groundlings in Los Angeles.

In Australia, Sandy has performed in leading theatre productions including: for Griffin: *Dogged*; for Belvoir St Theatre: *At What Cost?* (National Tour), *Light Shining in Buckinghamshire* and *Wayside Bride*; for Ilbijerri Theatre Company: *Body Armour*; for Sydney Theatre Company: *Stolen* and *Taboo*. Internationally, Sandy has performed for Seattle Children's Theatre Company in *Afternoon of the Elves*. Sandy's film and television credits include: for ABC: *The Messenger*; for Blossom Films: *The Last Anniversary*; for Omnilab Media, Ambience Entertainment, Film Victoria and Wales Creative IP Fund: *Killer Elite*; for Congaline Productions, EQ Media and Appleton Productions: *The Appleton Ladies Potato Race*.

As a playwright, Sandy wrote, produced, and performed her critically acclaimed one-woman show, *Matriarch* for which she won a Green Room Award for Best Actor and nominated for Best Writing in Independent Theatre. She is set to adapt *Matriarch* into a memoir with Echo Publishing.

Sandy recently produced and directed the environmental documentary film *Ngurra Muruy (Forest Camp)* and is the recipient of the 2024 NSW Environment Award for outstanding commitment and success in protecting Gumbaynggirr native forests and sacred sites.

ABOUT GRIFFIN

Griffin is the only theatre company in the country exclusively devoted to the development and staging of new Australian writing. Located in the historic SBW Stables Theatre, nestled in the heart of Kings Cross, Griffin has been Australia's home for the exploration of new stories since 1979.

We are the launch pad for new plays, ideas and writing that other theatres won't take a risk on. We boldly contribute to Australia's unique and powerful storytelling culture. Plays like *Prima Facie*, *Holding the Man* and *City of Gold* all had their world premieres at Griffin before going out to capture the national imagination. In the words of our longest-serving Artistic Director, **Ros Horin**:

"We are the theatre of first chances."

We are passionate about nurturing emerging and established practitioners alike. We pride ourselves on supporting our vast community of artists, audiences and supporters who consider our theatre their creative home. We help ambitious, bold, risk-taking and urgent Australian work get from the page onto the stage. We tell the stories that help us know who we are as a nation, and who we want to become.

Acknowledgement of Country

Griffin Theatre Company and the SBW Stables Theatre operate and tell stories on the unceded lands of the Gadigal of the Eora Nation. We acknowledge and honour Aboriginal and Torres Strait Islander people as the oldest continuous living culture on the planet, with more than 60,000 years of storytelling practice shaping and underpinning all aspects of Australian culture. It is a privilege that we do not take lightly: to work on this land, and to tell stories on its soil.

GRIFFIN THEATRE COMPANY
13 Craigend St
Gadigal Land, Kings Cross, NSW 2011

02 9332 1052
info@griffintheatre.com.au
griffintheatre.com.au

SBW STABLES THEATRE
10 Nimrod St
Gadigal Land, Kings Cross NSW 2011

BOOKINGS
griffintheatre.com.au
02 9361 3817

GRIFFIN FAMILY

Board
Bruce Meagher (Chair), Guillaume Babille, Nigel Barrington, Simon Burke AO, Julieanne Campbell, Jane Clifford, Declan Greene, Nakul Legha, Julia Pincus, Lenore Robertson AM, Simone Whetton

Artistic Director & co-CEO
Declan Greene

Executive Director & co-CEO
Julieanne Campbell

General Manager
Khym Scott

Administrator
Hayley Schmidt

Associate Artistic Director
Andrea James

Literary Manager
Dylan Van Den Berg

Literary Associate
Julian Larnach

Ticketing Manager
Sami Nelson

Ticketing Administrator
Nathan Harrison

Front of House Manager
Alex Bryant-Smith

Front of House
Riordan Berry, Kandice Joy, Max Philips, Maddy Withington, Willo Young

Head of Development
Jake Shavikin

Finance Manager
Chrissy Riley

Finance Consultant
Emma Murphy

Marketing Manager
Erica Penollar

Technical Manager
Sam Gray

Senior Producer
Emma Sampson

Associate Producer
Cassie Hamilton

Sustainability Coordinator
Sam Gray

Graphic Design
Susu Studio

Cover Photography
Daniel Grant

Publicist
Kabuku PR

Web Developer
DevQuoll

ABOUT CARRIAGEWORKS

Carriageworks is one of Australia's most renowned and significant contemporary creative industry hubs. We support artists and producers to develop and present major new works in performance, visual arts and related artforms. Reflecting the diverse communities of urban Sydney, our artist-led program is ambitious, radical and always inclusive.

CARRIAGEWORKS
Open Wed–Sun,
10am–5pm.

ADDRESS
245 Wilson St
Gadigal Land, Eveleigh, NSW 2015

CONTACTS
02 8571 9099
info@carriageworks.com.au
carriageworks.com.au

CARRIAGEWORKS STAFF

Board
Michael Gonski (Chair), Geoff Ainsworth AM, Andrew Maiden, Tony Nimac, Gitanjali Bhalla, Cameron Honey, Robi Stanton, Laura Berry, Jake Thomson

Chief Executive Officer
Fergus Linehan

Executive Assistant
Lucy Hallett

Head of People and Culture
Vicky Hopper

Director of Programming
Claire Hicks

Senior Curator, Visual Arts
Aarna Fitzgerald Hanley

Producer, Performance
Michelle Cao
Priyanka Martin
Tamar Kelly

Producer, Solid Ground
Felix May

Coordinator, Solid Ground
Tuneah Plumb

Solid Ground Education Assistant
Ray Baker

Head of Marketing and Communications
Miranda Cookman

Ticketing and CRM Manager
Ollie Lee

Communications Manager
Marissa Giannone

Digital Marketing Manager
Georgina Ryke

Head of Development
Camilla Chapman

Philanthropy and Sponsorships Manager
Cameron Brown

Ticketing Coordinator
Kaylee Rankin

Marketing Assistant
Jayce Carrano

Visitor Services Officer
Edmund Gock
Hannah Roberts

Director, Commercial and Partnerships
Andrew Demetriou

Commercial Account Manager
Hannah Spencer
Jacqueline De La Rosa Padilla
Emma Carson

Director of Production
Kri Leitner

Manager, Major Events
Chantel Bann

Producer, Events
Cynthia Loh

Visitor Experience Manager
Georgina Grisold

Production Manager
Dominic Hamra

Technical Manager
Colin Telfer

Technical Supervisor
Jared Wilson

Farmers Markets Creative Director
Mike McEnearney

Producer
Holly Bennett

Producer, Food Events
Jessica Abrahams

Assistant Producer, Food Events
Spencer Morrow

Head of Safety and Compliance
Jack Audas Preston

Finance and Administration Manager
Janine Peukert

Head of Finance
TingTing Li

Finance and Administrative Assistant
Eleanor McLeod
Alexandra-Cateluta Sava

Facilities Manager
William Brownley

Facilities Assistant
Rodrigo Arriaza

GRIFFIN DONORS

Income from Griffin activities covers less than 40% of our operating costs—leaving an ever-increasing gap for us to fill through government funding, sponsorship and the generosity of our individual supporters. Your support helps us bridge the gap and keep ticket prices affordable and our work at its best. To make a donation and a difference, contact Griffin on **(02) 9332 1101** or donate online at **griffintheatre.com.au**.

PROGRAM PATRONS

Griffin Ambassadors
Robertson Foundation

Griffin Amplify
Girgensohn Foundation

Griffin Literary Manager
Robertson Foundation

Griffin Redraft Fund
Shane & Cathryn Brennan

Suzie Miller Award
Suzie Miller

Griffin Studio
Gil Appleton
Darin Cooper Foundation
Kiong Lee & Richard Funston
Malcolm Robertson Foundation
Geoff & Wendy Simpson OAM
Danielle Smith & Sean Carmody

Griffin Studio Workshop
Shane & Cathryn Brennan (Patron)
Mary Ann Rolfe (Founding Patron)
Iolanda Capodanno & Juergen Krufczyk
Darin Cooper Foundation
Bob & Chris Ernst
Jane-Maree Hurley
Susan MacKinnon
Dianne & Peter O'Connell
Pip Rath & Wayne Lonergan
Jake Shavikin
Merilyn Sleigh & Raoul de Ferranti
Marina Grunstein Walking up the Hill Foundation

Griffin Women's Initiative
Katrina Barter
Jessica Block
Skye Bouvier
Julieanne Campbell
Iolanda Capodanno
Jane Clifford
Jennifer Darin
Lyndell Droga
Mandy Foley
Judith Fox & Yvonne Stewart
Melinda Graham
Sherry Gregory
Rosemary Hannah & Lynette Preston
Antonia Haralambis
Alexa Haslingden
Page Henty
Jane-Maree Hurley
Tessa Leong
Tory Loudon
Susan MacKinnon
Sophie McCarthy
Suzie Miller
Sam Mostyn
Naomi Parry
Julia Pincus
Ruth Ritchie
Lenore Robertson
Ann Sloan
Deanne Weir
Simone Whetton
Ali Yeldham
Anonymous (1)

PRODUCTION PARTNERS 2024

The Lewis Trilogy by Louis Nowra
Darin Cooper Foundation
Robert Dick & Erin Shiel
Rosemary Hannah & Lynette Preston
Richard McHugh & Kate Morgan
Bruce Meagher & Greg Waters
Julia Pincus & Ian Learmonth
Seaborn, Broughton & Walford Foundation

PRODUCTION PARTNERS 2023

Jailbaby by Suzie Miller
Lisa Barker & Don Russell
Darin Cooper Foundation
Robert Dick & Erin Shiel
Rachel Doyle
Danny Gilbert AM & Kathleen Gilbert
Rosemary Hannah & Lynette Preston
Richard McHugh & Kate Morgan
Bruce Meagher & Greg Waters
Julia Pincus & Ian Learmonth
Andrew Post & Susan Quill
Penelope Wass

SEASON DONORS

Company Patrons $100,000+
Shane & Cathryn Brennan
Neilson Foundation

Season Patrons $50,000+
Girgensohn Foundation
Robertson Foundation

Mainstage Donors $20,000+
Carla Zampatti Foundation
Darin Cooper Foundation
Robert Dick & Erin Shiel
Rosemary Hannah & Lynette Preston
Julia Pincus & Ian Learmonth
Mary Ann Rolfe
Sally Breen Family Foundation
The Wales Family Foundation
Anonymous (1)

Production Donors $10,000+
Rachel Doyle
Gordon & Marie Esden
Ingrid Kaiser
Richard McHugh & Kate Morgan
Bruce Meagher & Greg Waters
Suzie Miller
Mountain Air Foundation
Dianne & Peter O'Connell
Andrew Post & Susan Quill
Penelope Wass
The WeirAnderson Foundation

Rehearsal Donors $5,000–$9,999
Brian Abel & Mark Manton
Antoinette Albert
Gil Appleton
Lisa Barker & Don Russell
Ellen Borda
Bernard Coles
Ian Dickson
Danny Gilbert AM & Kathleen Gilbert
Libby Higgin & Gae Anderson
Elizabeth Hurst
Abraham & Helen James
The Keir Foundation
Lambert Bridge Foundation
Kiong Lee & Richard Funston
Catriona Morgan-Hunn
Anthony Paull
Rebel Penfold-Russell OAM
Pip Rath & Wayne Lonergan
In loving memory of Mary Ann Rolfe
Geoff & Wendy Simpson OAM
The Sky Foundation
Merilyn Sleigh & Raoul de Ferranti
Danielle Smith & Sean Carmody

Rehearsal Donors $5,000–$9,999 Continued.
Adam Suckling
Marina Grunstein Walking Up the Hill Foundation
Anonymous (1)

Final Draft Donors $3,000–$4,999
Melissa Ball
Iolanda Capodano & Juergen Krufczyk
Corinne & Bryan
Bob & Chris Ernst
Sherry Gregory
Kate Harrison
James Hartwright & Kerrin D'Arcy
John Head
Jane-Maree Hurley
Susan MacKinnon
Don & Leslie Parsonage
Elizabeth Wing

Workshop Donors $1,000–$2,999
Baly Douglass Foundation
Katrina Barter
Cherry & Peter Best
Jessica Block
Skye Bouvier
Christy Boyce & Madeleine Beaumont
Stephen & Annabelle Burley
Julieanne Campbell
Susie Carleton
Anna Cleary
Jane Clifford
Brian Everingham
John & Libby Fairfax
Mandy Foley
Hon Ben Franklin MLC
Robert Furley
Jennifer Giles
Global Creatures
Nicky Gluyas
Melinda Graham
Peter Graves
Peter Gray & Helen Thwaites
Mink Greene
Kate Halliday
Antonia Haralambis
Alexa Haslingden
Page Henty
Mark Hopkinson & Michelle Opie
Michael Jackson
David & Adrienne Kitching
Benjamin Law
Tessa Leong
Richard & Elizabeth Longes
Tory Loudon
Helen Lynch AM & Helen Bauer
Patricia Lynch
Kyrsty Macdonald & Christopher Hazell
Prudence Manrique
Kate Richardson & Chris Marrable
Sophie McCarthy
John McCallum & Jenny Nicholls
Sam Mostyn
Ian Neuss & Penny Young
David Nguyen
Naomi Parry
Shaan Perera
Ian Phipps
Martin Portus
Steve Rietoff
In memory of Katherine Robertson
Sylvia Rosenblum
Jake Shavikin
Jann Skinner
Ann & Quinn Sloan
Geoffrey Starr
Leslie Stern
Sue Thomson
Janet Wahlquist
Richard Weinstein & Richard Benedict
Simone Whetton
Rob White & Lisa Hamilton
Ali Yeldham
Anonymous (4)

Reading Donors $500–$999
Nicole Abadee & Rob Macfarlan
Brian Abel
Robyn Ayres
Claire Bornhoffen
Tim Capelin
Jane Christensen
Amanda Clark
David Davies
Michael Diamond & Georgina F
Max Dingle OAM
Elizabeth Diprose
Sue Donnelly
Alan Froude & David Round
David Hoskins & Paul McKnight
Nicki Jam
Mira Joksovic
Matt Jones & Rebecca Bourne Jones
Greg Lamont & Gerard Wilmann
Rosemary Lucas & Robert Yuen
Ian & Elizabeth MacDonald
Robert Marks
Dr Stephen McNamara
Jacqui Mercer
Patricia Novikoff
Virginia Pursell
Nick Read
A.O. Redmond
Gemma Rygate
Rob & Rae Spence
Catherine Sullivan & Alexandra Bowen
Elizabeth Thompson
Mike Thompson
Ariadne Vromen
David & Jennifer Watson
Julie Whitfield
Anonymous (2)

First Draft Donors $200–$499
Priscilla Adey
Elizabeth Antonievich
Edwina Birch
David Caulfield
Sue Clark
Amanda Connelly
Edward Cooper & Daniel Zucker
Bryan Cutler
Elizabeth Evatt
Robyn Fortescue & Rosie Wagstaff
Jock Given
Deane Golding
Wendy Gray
Jan Harland
Raewyn Harlock
Robert Henderson & Marijke Conrade
Sylvia Hrovatin
Matthew Huxtable
Andrew Inglis
James Landon-Smith
Anna Logan
Norman Long
Noella Lopez
George & Maruschka Loupis
Louise McDonald
Duncan McKay
Margaret Murphy
Carolyn Newman
Peter Pezzutti
Belinda Piggott & David Ojerholm
Christopher Powell
Ann Rocca
Michael & Noelleen Rosen
Catherine Rothery
Kevin & Shirley Ryan
Dimity Scales
Julia Selby
James, Beu & Sue
Margaret Teh
Samantha Turley
Adam Van Rooijen
Eve Wynhausen
William Zappa
Anonymous (3)

Griffin Friends Forever
We remember and honour those who have generously supported the future of Australian storytelling through a bequest to Griffin Theatre Company

Thank you:
Annette Mary Lunney
Estate of the Late John William Roe

CURRENT AS OF 15 JUNE 2024

GRIFFIN SPONSORS

Griffin would like to thank the following:

OUR PARTNERS

GOVERNMENT SUPPORTERS

PATRON

LEGACY BENEFACTOR

CREATIVE PARTNERS

COMPANY PARTNERS

Griffin Theatre Company is assisted by the Australian Government through Creative Australia, its principal arts investment and advisory body.

www.ingramcontent.com/pod-product-compliance
Lightning Source LLC
Chambersburg PA
CBHW050021090426
42734CB00021B/3371